This book belongs to

There's a Beetle in My Bucket

and other challenges facing an orphaned horse

by
Heather Rosselle Irwin

Author: Heather Rosselle Irwin
Cover Designer: Jennifer Tipton Cappoen
Editor: Lynn Bemer Coble

PCJunior is an imprint of **Paws and Claws Publishing, LLC.**
1589 Skeet Club Road, Suite 102 #175
High Point, NC 27265
www.PawsandClawsPublishing.com
info@pawsandclawspublishing.com

ISBN # 978-1-946198-17-4
Printed in the United States

Acknowledgements

Much love and thanks go out to my sweet husband Hugh. He has supported me in every way along this journey. He knows how much I love to write and to share my animal stories with people.

He's patient and knows how many irons I have in the fire at times. It's during these overwhelming times that he brings me back to earth and makes me feel human again.

If I need it (and he seems to know whenever I do), his advice is endless. He definitely knows of my love for animals, and his is just as strong. Our family currently consists of two dogs, four cats, four horses, and one miniature donkey. If we could have more, we definitely would! My grandmother, Zella (aka 'Nanny'), always said, "Where there is love, there is room."

Speaking of Nanny, she taught me the importance of how to treat people with kindness and love. She taught me many lessons, without her even realizing it. I watched her interact with family members and friends as a young girl, and I wanted to be just like her when I grew up. She was a beautiful woman inside and out. She was one of the kindest women I've ever met. I was so blessed to have her in my life.

To the sweet angel in my life, my stepmother Linda. I was never thrilled about that title. She's really the "mother of my heart."

Over 30 years ago, she started filling my life with love and encouragement in many ways. I've never known anyone like her and probably never will again.

A very special thank you to Linda for her continued interest in my writing and in this book in particular. I'm thankful that she read the story and that her excitement and enthusiasm helped keep me on track.

To my father Donald who encouraged me to follow my heart and to do what made me happy in this life. He wanted me to go to college, even though I was apprehensive. He said to at least try it and that if I didn't want to continue, I could do something else.

He always encouraged me to try different things. And then he followed up by saying that if I ended up selling pencils on the street, that was okay, as long as it made me happy. When he said that to me as a child, I didn't know exactly what he meant. But as I progressed through my life, his words of wisdom made much more sense. "Do what makes you happy."

To this day, I thank him for my willingness to take chances, even if those efforts made me uncomfortable at times.

To my mother Virginia, who brought me into this world where I was able to grow up and to make many choices in my life. Not all of those choices were good ones, but she always supported me in a loving manner, no matter what.

Thank you to her for her sense of humor and for the laughter we've shared along the way.

She always wanted what was best for me and guided me toward those things. She still does to this day. For all of these things, I say a heartfelt thank you to her.

To my older and only brother Curtis, who was my sidekick in our adventures as we looked for little animals and creatures in the creeks and throughout the woods behind our house.

We're siblings and friends. We all need friends now and then. He was always there for me when we were growing up and is to this day.

We both also share a love of animals.

He has an incredible sense of humor, which is always welcomed in our world today. Thank you for making me laugh, Brother, and for your support all along the way.

To my aunt Patty, who was involved in my life quite a bit while I was a young girl. I was able to spend a lot of time with her during the summer months and during most Christmas celebrations. She gave me my first horse book for Christmas one year.

I remember how excited I was and that the book had a lot of beautiful pictures, which was important at my young age.

Spending time with her was special and formed the bond we have today.

To my grandmother June and grandfather John. They had a very old typewriter that they kept on the floor in the foyer closet. They must have thought it was much too heavy to put anywhere up high. I was about five years old when I first discovered it back in the dark corner of the closet. Immediately I dragged it across the floor toward the light and started to tap away on it. After that, every visit with them included some time sitting on the floor with that old typewriter, writing notes, letters, and stories about simple things. Thank you to the two of them from their writer-in-the-making!

Dedication

This book is dedicated to my father, Donald. He had wonderful gifts for writing and storytelling. Without my realization of it, he passed some of those gifts on to me. During his life, he shared stories that impacted me, both positively and negatively.

After he retired, he wrote a collection of short stories that I'm certain would have been published if he had taken that next step. His hesitation to try and get his stories published gave me the strength and confidence to seek the publication of Sequoyah's story.

I am happy to say that his belief in God, experiences, tough love, and lessons made me the woman whom I am today.

Prologue

I was a horse. A very different horse. I didn't realize this for quite some time, because I never met my real mother. I had difficulties knowing how I was supposed to act and how to behave as a horse. I was scared of a lot of things because I didn't have a horse to teach me what was normal and what was not.

In fact, I went through a lot of obstacles and encountered many problems that a normal horse would not usually experience.

I remember one time when I was eating by myself for the first time. I was so proud, and my adoptive human mommy was proud of me too! She watched me approach my little yellow feed bucket proudly on my own. I put my nose in the bucket and suddenly jumped back about ten feet. I made the loudest, scariest sound either one of us has ever heard. There was a shiny black thing in my bucket, and I was scared beyond belief. My mommy looked into that bucket and saw that it was a big black beetle moving around in my feed. Apparently it had fallen in there by mistake and couldn't get out. Mommy pulled the beetle out with her hand and showed me that it wasn't anything to be afraid of at all. She let me see it up close, and she even let me smell it. Only then did I realize that it wasn't scary. I had overreacted.

That was only one of many things I had to learn as a baby orphaned horse. I know I would have learned that eventually with my real herd of horses, but I was so happy to have learned about it from my human mommy.

I was going to experience many things like that in the future as I grew up as an orphan. I think I was ready for my life. I had a lot of support from my human mommy. But my life was still going to be filled with ups and downs along the way. However I was ready!

All You Need

is Love

...and a Horse.

~Author Unknown

Chapter One

My life started in a cold, white field all by myself. I looked around and all that I saw were a lot of leafless tall trees and white fluffy stuff everywhere I could see. Later I was told that the white stuff was *snow* and that it always covers the ground during a certain time of the year.

Apparently the snow had fallen on my first day here on earth. I didn't mind too much because I was happy to see the sunshine and the little birds and other animals romping around near me. Even though I was cold and had very little hair to keep me warm, I was happy to be here and lucky to be alive!

I found out later that my chances for survival weren't very good. I will tell you more about that later in my story.

I had so many questions. My first one was, *Where was I?*

Where was everyone else that looked like me? I felt kind of alone in this big field covered with snow.

I was really cold, but I didn't particularly know why. I was a bit wet and needed drying off, but no one was around to help me with that either. I looked around and waited. I even took a little nap when I could.

You never knew what the future held, I thought to myself as I waited and napped. I had to get my rest while I could. I felt as if I had been through a lot that day, but I didn't really know what it was that had happened. I saw a bigger version of me walking around, but it never came over to say hello.

The brightness in the sky started to turn a little bit gray and the air around me felt different. I was still cold and had become hungry, but other things were happening.

All of a sudden, I heard noises that got louder by the minute. I looked all around to see what might be making those noises. I was scared but also a bit curious. *What was this thing, and why was it coming closer to me? Was it going to hurt me?* It surely didn't look like me and didn't smell like me. *But why didn't it, and what in the world was it?*

I just lay there and didn't move, hoping it wouldn't notice me and would keep moving. A few moments later, I found myself being picked up off the white cold stuff and being carried into a dry metal box on wheels. Later I found out that this was called a *trailer* and was used to move things like me safely around from place to place.

"Wow," I said to myself, "I think I'm in for a really big adventure!"

Let a Horse
Whisper in your ear
and breathe on
your Heart.
You will never regret it.

~Author Unknown

Chapter Two

Well, this was quite a ride, I thought. But what was really neat was that I wasn't alone in the box on wheels. There was this being that stayed with me from the moment I was carried from the snowy field and laid gently into the moving box. This being never left my side, and it comforted me as the box moved. It covered me with a soft blanket that made me feel warm. It dried me off too.

Much later I found out that this being was my human, my person, my caretaker, my mother, or whatever you want to call it. From her first touch, I liked the feeling of her gentle comfort. But I was confused that she didn't look a thing like me. I had four legs, and she seemed to have only two. I definitely had way more hair than her. However, even though that was the case, she wasn't shivering and I was.

Boy, I hoped these beings would take me somewhere warm!

The trip in the moving box on wheels was short. After the box stopped, I was quickly carried out of it and placed into a larger, more comfortable heated box.

I'm not sure what that heated box was, but it was nice and comfortable. I was laid down on a soft floor and kept warm by a blanket that these creatures placed over me.

Later I found out that these creatures were called *humans* and this second "heated box" that I was placed into was called a *stall*. My stall was one of many in this larger box that I found out was called a *barn*. It had smells that I liked and that I seemed to be familiar with in some way. The barn smelled like me. And in the barn, I could hear sounds nearby that I was starting to make myself. I had my very own stall in a barn that kept me warm. Whatever all this was, it was working out just fine for me as far as I could tell.

Something told me that I should be outdoors. That was *instinct*. But that same something told me that I was different from most creatures like me. I believed that I was going to be a different and very special kind of horse.

Yes, I said, "Horse!" Every creature—no matter what it is— knows what it is when it is born. That's called *instinct* and every creature has it. I was a horse and the being taking good care of me was a human. That much I understood.

I started to get warm as my humans gathered around me. As it turned out, I was born in the wintertime during a snowstorm.

But once I was found in the snowy field, my human started taking care of me the best that she could.

However, I was hungry and didn't feel very well. *Where was my horse mommy with some nutrition for me?* I wondered. Later I found out that my horse mommy didn't have any milk for me because she couldn't produce it for some reason. My first meal after birth was very important, and I didn't get it from my real mommy. My first meal was supposed to give me a lot of vitamins and other things that would help me stay healthy and prevent me from getting sick as a baby. My horse mommy's milk was supposed to give me the help that I needed to start my life as a healthy horse. I never got that assistance from her. Because of that, I wasn't feeling well by that time.

My human knew what was happening and called in more humans to give me the help that I needed. I was given something to make me feel better and hopefully to help me live through this whole ordeal. Yes, apparently this was a very serious situation. My life depended on that first meal with medicine added to it that those humans fed to me. I had started my life at a grave disadvantage. At that point, I needed all the help I could get in order to survive and live a long and healthy life.

I heard my human—whom I later found out was called Heather—talking to another human who was called a *veterinarian*. A veterinarian was a doctor who took care of animals.

I heard them refer to me as an *orphan*.

An orphan? I thought I was a horse. Then I was really confused. Well, I found out that I was indeed a horse. But because my real horse mommy couldn't take care of me, I was considered an orphan. An orphaned horse. *What was I to think of that?* I really didn't know at that point.

I guessed I would just trust in Heather and her human friends to help guide me in the right direction and to keep me safe and healthy.

The Horse
can transform
the Human Spirit
into Wind...

~Author Unknown

Chapter 3

A couple of weeks went by, and I was starting to feel much better and stronger. In fact, I was standing on my own four hooves. I was even taking steps without falling down a lot. And I had been falling down often before. With a little help from Heather, I was able to stand up and steady myself for a few seconds. She put her hands under me and helped me get started. Then I took a step forward and very quickly fell down. Luckily for me, there was a lot of soft stuff to land on so I didn't get hurt.

As the walking lessons continued, I got better and better at it. I started to walk without falling down! I walked in circle after circle until I got tired and needed to rest. I think Heather was proud of me because she had the biggest smile on her face.

As I mentioned earlier, during my first few days on earth, the animal doctor gave me some medicine and milk with vitamins

in it. I also got a lot of help from Heather and her human friends. I felt as if I was getting stronger by the day. I think that's why I could finally take the tiny steps and walk in those big circles. All the humans fed me milk out of a bottle frequently throughout each day and night. They always kept me warm.

I guess if my horse mommy were here, she would've done the same thing for me. Well, since it looked like I was never going to meet my horse mommy, I decided to call Heather my mommy instead.

She seemed to have taken to me and was quite fond of me. I felt the love that she had for me. It was probably similar to the love my horse mommy would have had for me.

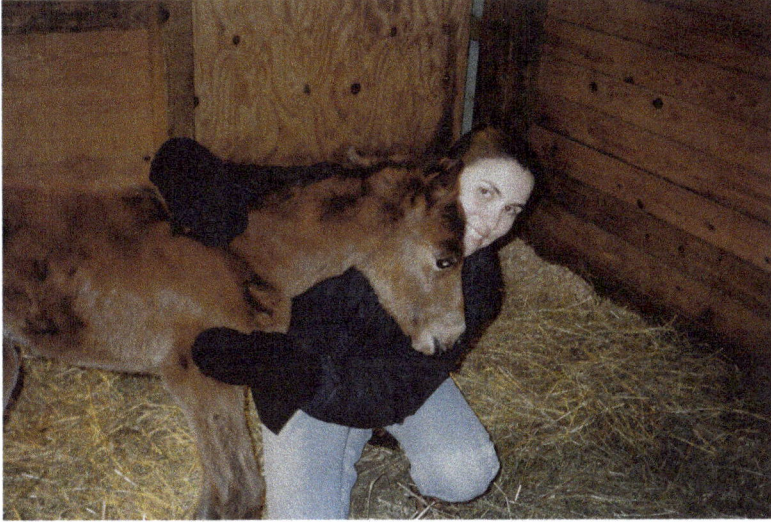

As Heather was working with me in my stall, she was so excited when I was able to stand up on my own. She exclaimed, "How wonderful it is to see you standing, Sequoyah!"

How wonderful what? What did she call me? What was a Sequoyah? I looked around the stall and nobody else was there except for her and me. Was my name Sequoyah? I wondered. She was called Heather and I must have been called Sequoyah. I liked it.

🪲 🪲 🪲

The longer I got to hang around and get to know my mommy, I found out why she gave me that name. You see, Heather was part American Indian and she was very proud of her heritage. My name just so happened to be an Indian name. She was proud of her family and her heritage, and she was also proud of me. She wanted to give me a great and important name. *Sequoyah* was a Cherokee Native American who created an alphabet for the Cherokee language. He used this alphabet to record the history of his tribe. *I'd say that he was important.*

Heather and I spent a lot of time together, and she talked to me a lot. Some of what she said I understood and some of it, I didn't. She told me that American Indians thought that horses were a gift from above. They held horses in very high esteem, and horses represented power in Native American tribes.

I could see that things were going to be different with this type of mommy. I could sense that there were some things that would be a challenge for both of us. That was okay, because life was full of challenges and it was those challenges that made us stronger!

Chapter 4

It was a very cold winter and I was affected by the cold because I didn't have a horse mommy to keep me warm. I was much too small to go outdoors and meet the other horses that I could hear from my stall. They might have tried to keep me warm, but they also might have stepped on me because I was so small and they didn't know me yet.

Heather—who was getting to know me well—used a heat lamp in my stall and a blanket when I was lying down to keep me warm. But sometimes the conditions made me shiver and made me uncomfortable anyway. Heather and her friends came up with a new idea to keep me warm and comfortable until the weather turned more conducive for me. They put me in the basement of Heather's friends' home with bedding material for me to lie down on when I got tired. That was great! By simply walking down the stairs, they could check on me anytime.

Heather visited me frequently at her friends' home. She came downstairs and worked with me on some skills that my horse mommy would've taught me if she were there. She taught me about staying out of her space and not crowding her. I wanted to be in her space because I loved her so much. Also until she taught me, I didn't know any better.

She taught me that if I got too close, I might step on her and hurt her by accident. That actually happened quite a bit, until I finally understood. She taught me to pay attention to her when she was talking to me. That was tough for me because I was such a daydreamer. I was smart and paid attention to her, but I really wanted to do my own thing. I've heard some humans call this hardheaded, but Heather told me that I was super smart and knew what I wanted. I liked her explanation better than the hardheaded one.

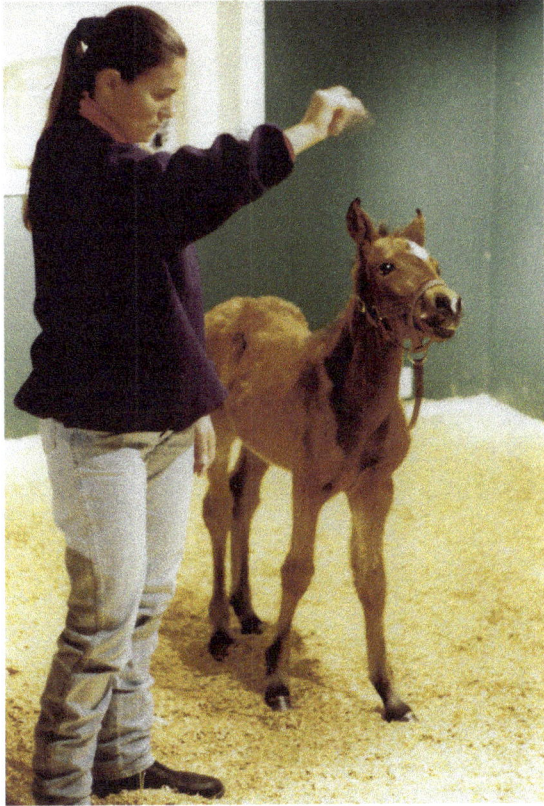

Heather and I had a lot of little talks on the side about my behavior. Both good and not-so-good behavior.

All of our talks were educational and productive. Even though I was a daydreamer, I learned a lot from her and her other humans.

Chapter 5

As the days passed, things about my body were changing. My hair was getting longer and my legs were getting stronger. I was eager to get out of their basement and back into my own stall in the barn. I had grown tall enough that I could see out the basement window and could see that there were creatures that looked like me out there. They had four legs just like me. I could see them doing what I should be doing then and in the future. Things were looking bright for me.

Mommy did in fact move me outdoors and back to the barn to my own stall. She wanted me to get some fresh air and also wanted to see how I moved around in the great outdoors. It really looked different out there. I also got to meet some new friends that had four legs like me. That was about all that we had in common. They had these pointy things on their heads and made odd noises. Heather explained to me that they were called

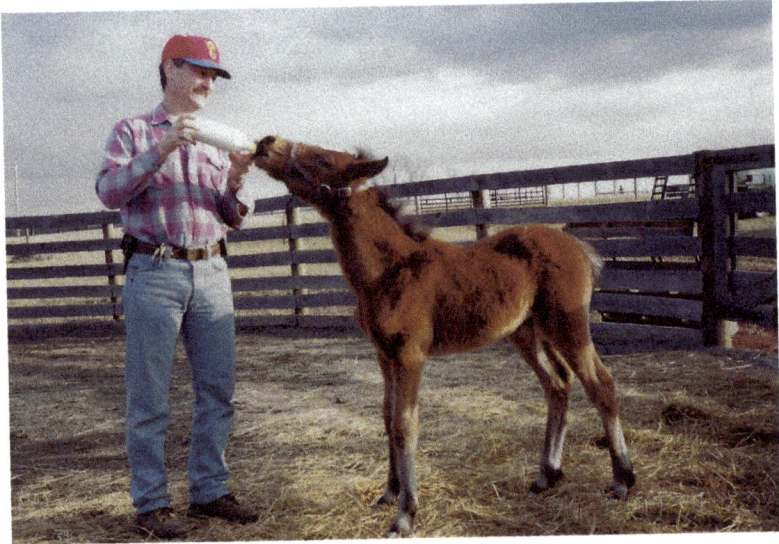

goats and were friendly little creatures. Nevertheless, they quickly became my friends and companions when my mommy wasn't with me. We kept each other company, which was important. Heather explained to me that I always needed a friend to be with and that I needed to be a good friend to them as well. That was great advice that I'd remember.

Since it was still a little bit cold outdoors, Mommy got me a blanket to wear to make sure I was comfortable. It looked a lot like the one she wore when she was outdoors with me. It had buckles and buttons and stayed really snug on me. At first it was a little bit big, but I grew into it in no time at all.

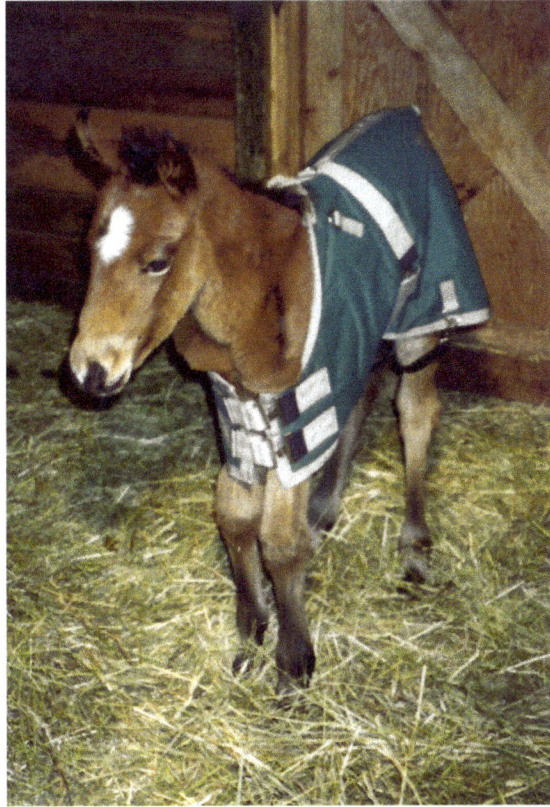

I started to walk around the grassy area. Then all of a sudden, I burst into what humans call a *trot* and then into a full-out run. Wow, that was fun! I didn't know I could do that. Most of the time, I was in a smaller space and just walked around. Then I was *running!* In fact, my mommy could hardly keep up with me. She tried to run by my side, but I took off without her. If she were a horse like me, she could have kept up. But I had an advantage. I had four legs and she only had two. Well, that was *one* way we were different.

As time went on, I was discovering more differences between my mommy and me. I was finding out how my life as an orphaned horse was going to be a challenge, to say the least. I was starting to have some fun with this outdoors-in-the-yard thing. I was able to kick, buck, and stand on my hind legs when I was by my mommy's side, but she seemed scared of me when I did those things. They seemed natural to me, but apparently they were dangerous for her. She explained to me that one day soon, the other horses would teach me when it was and was not appropriate to do those things.

Another thing I did—which was not appropriate—was to grab certain things with my mouth. I was simply curious and wanted to see how things felt. I tried that on my mommy's hand

one time. She quickly moved it and sternly told me, "No!" Boy, was I ever in trouble! Again, she explained to me that the other "four-leggeds" like me would probably have reacted similarly. But they also might have bitten me back. The reason I did that to my mommy's hand was that I was looking for the bottle of milk that had been attached to her hand at one time.

I had a lot to learn. I was starting to get the idea that if I were spending time with other horses, they would teach me how a baby horse like me should behave itself. I knew that Mommy was doing the best she could. But she wasn't a horse and I wasn't a human. It was as simple as that.

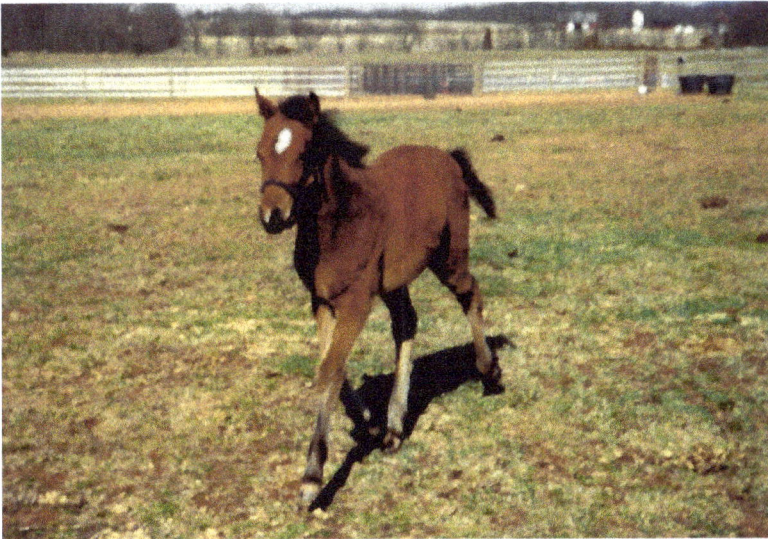

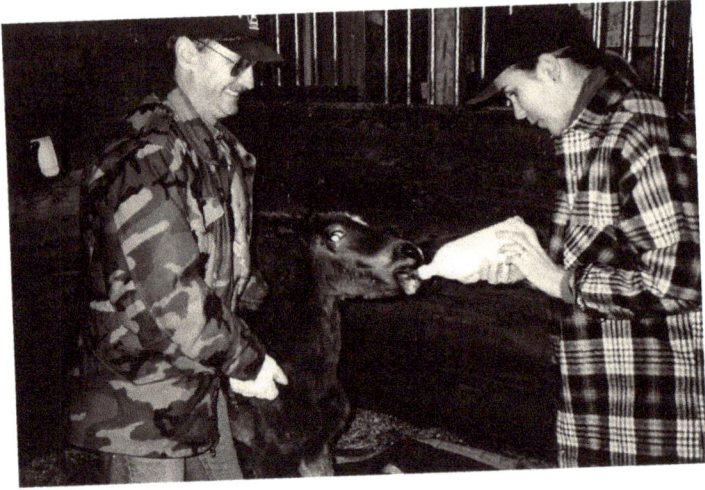

Chapter 6

My person—whom I knew as my human mommy—had a special person of her own. I found out that she called him "Hugh." He was often by her side and helped her with me a lot.

I could see why, because I surely could be a handful at times. You see, as I said before, she was a human and I was a horse. There were times when I didn't know the difference, and those were the times when I became a handful and a real challenge.

I followed Heather around everywhere. When I wasn't sleeping, I wanted to run and play with her all the time. That involved kicking, bucking, rearing, and running. Sometimes I kicked my legs in her direction, as I mentioned earlier. I've noticed that she didn't kick back at me, but I really needed her to do something in order for me to know what was acceptable and what was not. I needed to know where I stood in her "herd."

She and her human, Hugh, were trying to figure me out and I was trying to figure them out as well. Our behaviors were much different and I needed to be taught how to act like a horse, not a human. That was confusing to me.

Apparently there were certain things that only a mommy horse could teach a baby horse. I heard Heather and Hugh talking about that in the barn one day. I was going to need special care as I grew up so that I'd understand that I was a horse.

Chapter 7

Several months have gone by and I have changed even more. I was taller, stronger, and faster than ever! I learned to eat on my own without the help of my human. I had my own feed bucket and I no longer needed to be fed from a bottle. It looked as though my humans were happy about that.

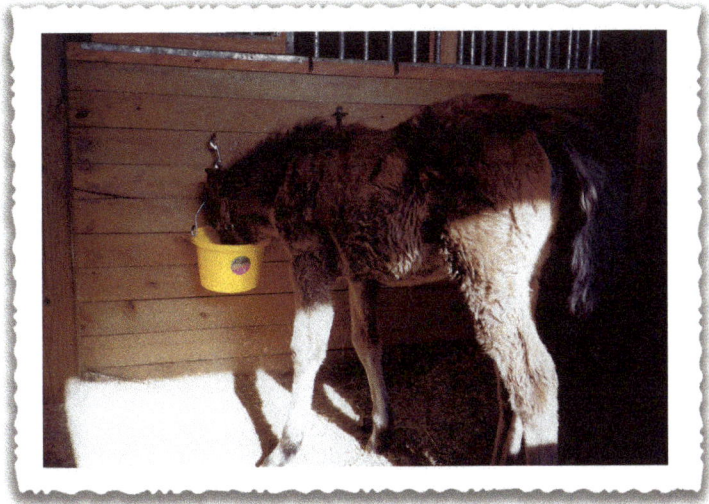

Speaking of my humans, Heather and Hugh have let me go out and play with the other horses, since I was finally stronger. I learned so much from them. The horses have taught me how to behave like a horse. When I did something that wasn't quite right in their world, they certainly let me know. For instance, I learned that if I got too close to them when I wasn't welcomed, they pushed me away a little bit.

My human mommy, Heather, had this same problem with me. But since I had gotten bigger, she could only push me away so much. This was still a confusing time for me since my mommy was human and I needed to behave like a horse. This was my biggest challenge by far. I knew there were going to be a lot more lessons in the future. It was going to take a lot of patience on my part and Heather's part. But the bottom line was that I loved her and I knew she loved me, so our life together was going to be a good one.

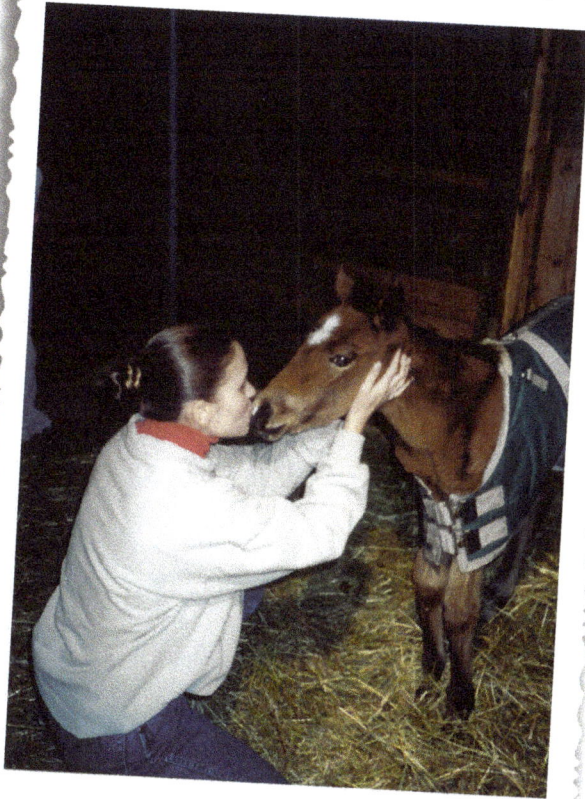

A true Horseman does not look at the Horse with his eyes, he looks at his Horse with his Heart.

~Author Unknown

Chapter 8

It was summertime and I didn't need my blanket anymore. I've lost some of my hair, which I thought was normal for me. All the other horses have lost some of their hair too, so I must have been healthy and normal. By then, I wasn't sure I'd ever entirely feel like a normal horse, but I was trying to fit in the best I could.

Heather and Hugh decided it was time to move me from my original barn home where I started my life to their barn at their farm, so I could live closer to them. They wanted me close so we could be together more often. They lived about a mile down the road. Unfortunately, that meant I wasn't going to see my horse friends anymore. They were busy teaching me to be what I was: a horse! This move was going to make things different again, but I trusted that Heather and Hugh knew what they were doing. I'll tell you, being a not-so-normal horse was sure tough. This whole orphan thing was confusing.

After the move to Heather and Hugh's farm, I didn't have anybody around that looked like me. *Who was going to teach me and continually test my horse skills?* Well, I guessed it was back to acting like a human again.

One morning Heather walked out into the field to greet me and to see how I was adjusting to my new home. She was talking to me, but I surely didn't know what she was saying. Her voice was low and sweet, and I think she asked me if I were hungry and ready for my breakfast. Well, I don't know exactly what happened next. But all of a sudden, I got scared by something and jumped directly toward Heather! She was startled at my reaction, which occurred because a big bird flew overhead. She jumped as well, but not in time to get out of my way. I accidentally stepped on her foot, and she let out the biggest noise I had ever heard! She scolded me soundly, but I didn't understand that at all.

Later she followed up by telling me that if I had done that to another horse, I probably would have been kicked and would have quickly learned my lesson.

After that, I noticed that Heather was walking differently. And it occurred to me that I had really hurt her. She told me that a small bone in her foot was broken. But I didn't know what that meant. What I *did* understand was that I needed to give Heather

her personal space so I didn't hurt her again.

Once again, since Heather was a human, she couldn't teach me the things I needed to know to grow up as a normal horse. I guess the lesson I learned with that incident was that if I got scared by something, I shouldn't jump on top of my human or another horse. Instead I should respect their space and move away from them. That way I wouldn't hurt them.

To ride on a

Horse

is to fly without

Wings

~Author Unknown

Chapter 9

Well, as time passed, Heather did her best to teach me what I needed to know. We still had little issues here and there, but I was learning from her and she was learning from me. She would sit out in the field watching me and holding what I later learned was a *book*. She did that quite often and I think she used those books to understand me better. I wished someone had published a book that horses could use to learn about humans.

One day I heard Heather telling Hugh that I needed another horse to be with me, not only to teach me how to act properly, but also to be a companion. *Oh boy, I got to have a horse friend again!* It took a couple of months for them to find just the right one to be with me, but they finally did. Her name was Ellie and

she was a miniature version of me. She sort of looked like me, but some things were different. Her ears were really long and her hair looked different from mine. She was half my size and she didn't make the same noises I made.

When Ellie was introduced into my pasture, I heard Mommy say that she was a donkey. I had met a donkey at my first home, so I was a little bit familiar with them. The fact that she was a donkey and not a horse explained the long ears for sure. And the sounds that came out of that mouth were very different from mine.

Apparently Mommy thought a donkey would be a good companion and would protect me. She was right. We were by each other's side all the time, and nothing came into our pasture that wasn't supposed to be there. Ellie pinned her ears back and chased any animal that came in without an invitation. She protected me from dogs, cats, and wild animals that came into our space and could potentially hurt us.

I knew from the very start that we were going to be the best of friends.

To many, the words Love, Hope and Dreams are Synonymous with Horses.

~Author Unknown

Chapter 10

Life was really good on this farm with Heather and Hugh. I was growing taller and having fun with my little friend, Ellie. I noticed that she wasn't growing tall like me. She seemed healthy and playful and did all the things I did, but she just wasn't seeming to grow tall. I saw a lot of horses in my first home that were different colors and sizes, but none that were as little as Ellie. I decided not to give it another thought when I heard Heather and Hugh talking about her and how cute she was. I heard them say, "Miniature donkey," in one of their conversations. They talked about her as if that were as big as she would get. There was a donkey in my herd at my first home, but she was bigger. After their conversation, I knew that Ellie was a miniature version of her. There was nothing wrong with Ellie at all. She was going to stay cute and little her whole life. And I would be tall and pretty

my whole life. I knew this because I heard Mom and Dad talking about us.

"It takes all kinds of horses to make the world go around," they said.

Speaking of Mom and Dad, I also heard them talking about moving down south to live. They said the winters wouldn't be as cold as they were up here and, apparently, they had family down there.

I told Ellie about what I had heard, and we both agreed that we would be happy to have a change in our lives too. We liked it where we lived, but we only had a limited space where we could run and play. Mommy said they were looking at moving to a farm that was bigger than this one.

As Ellie and I were communicating, she asked me if I thought we were going to move south with them. I told Ellie that Mommy and Daddy were my best friends. I knew I was a horse and they were humans, but I felt as though I was part human too. I wasn't sure I could change the way I felt since I spent more time with them than with horses when I was younger. I guess what I was trying to tell my little friend, Ellie, was that surely they wouldn't leave me behind.

That got me thinking more and more about their move. I was

hoping they would take us with them. I heard them talking about selling a house and about moving a car and some furniture. But I didn't hear anything about Ellie and me. *Where else would we go if they didn't take us with them?* I heard them say that the trip to get where they wanted to live would take about six hours. I couldn't walk for six hours, and I knew that Ellie couldn't walk that far with her short legs! I didn't think there was enough room in their little metal box on wheels for us.

I needed to stop worrying and to start thinking positive thoughts. I told Ellie to do the same. Worrying would get us nowhere. It was time for dinner, so I was going to enjoy my oats and hay and quit thinking about all this talk about moving for a while.

A Horse
is Poetry
in Motion

~Author Unknown

Chapter 11

Ellie and I woke up to another beautiful morning in Virginia, which is where we lived. Both of us were concerned that this was where we were going to be left behind when Mommy and Daddy moved to North Carolina. We've heard chatter about the move and the plans for it over the past couple of months, but nothing has been said about us going with them. *Was this how things were going to go? When our family moved from one state to another, would they take us horses with them? Or would we stay where we were?*

I seemed to remember way back when I was only two days old when my mommy put me in a metal box on wheels. When it moved, it shook and rattled while I was in there. Thank goodness Mommy was in there with me to comfort me. I remembered when it stopped moving and they opened the door of the box,

which I later learned was called a *horse trailer*. I was in a totally different place from where I started. As I looked around our current farm, I didn't see a horse trailer anywhere. If Ellie and I were taken on a trip to another state, we would need one of those for sure. I became even more worried that we wouldn't be making the trip with them.

Mommy and Daddy had boxes with wheels that they moved around in, but I didn't see one for us. *Were they going to find another home for us instead of moving us to their new farm? I wondered. Would they take me back to where I started my orphaned life? Were we going to be overlooked and forgotten?* I knew my mind was going a mile a minute worrying about this, but I loved Heather and Hugh and always wanted to be with them. *But did they feel the same way about Ellie and me? Did they not love me because I was different from most horses that actually had a horse for a mommy?*

I tried really hard to behave and to please Heather and Hugh. But sometimes I messed up, because I didn't completely know how to act like a horse. I also looked a little different from a horse that was brought up by her real mommy. I almost didn't survive when I was very young because I didn't get my real mommy's milk. That lack of milk from her stunted my growth, and I looked a little different from other horses. But Heather always told me that it was what was on the inside that mattered. I had a big heart with lots of love to give. I always whinnied when I saw my

favorite people. That was my way of saying, "Hello," and "How are you?"

Heather and Hugh certainly acted like they loved us. They took care of us, fed us, brushed us, took lots of pictures of us, and occasionally played in the field with us. I was two years old at that point, and those two years had allowed us to share a lot of history, training, and memories. Surely they wouldn't want to just throw all of that away. All Ellie and I could do was wait and see what would happen.

Our family also included a dog and two cats. I've heard them talk about putting them in their box on wheels and carrying them down the road. But again, I've heard nothing about the two of us. *If only I could talk to them and tell them how badly I wanted to go with them on this move.* I couldn't imagine being without my people. Don't get me wrong. I loved my little friend, Ellie. But Heather and Hugh were my first loves and the ones who saved my life when I was a baby.

As the sun set once again, I thought about what was to come and what kind of life Ellie and I would have in the future. As the stars came out on that clear night, I stared at them and held onto hope for all of us to stay together as a family.

A good Rider can
hear his Horse
speak to him.
A great Rider can hear
his Horse Whisper.

~Author Unknown

Chapter 12

Well, it was a new day and it was beautiful outdoors. The birds were chirping and the little wildflowers were starting to bloom. I didn't know what it was, but somehow things seemed a little different around home today. It seemed as if something were about to happen.

Then I remembered the move. Oh yeah, that. I tried to put it out of my mind.

Ellie and I ate our morning oats and hay as usual. Afterward we started moving around our pasture as we normally do to check things out. We heard the gate in the fence open. It wasn't an unusual sound. Heather or Hugh was probably going to top off the water in our water trough. I thought it was supposed to be a warm day, and we tended to drink a lot of water on those days.

As it turned out, it was Heather coming into our pasture.

She didn't go to the water trough, but instead went to the room where she kept our supplies. We had a special room where she stored oats, treats, halters and lead lines, and all the other things we needed as a horse and a donkey. Ellie and I were naturally curious, so we wandered over to say hi and watched what she was doing in there.

She started packing all our things into a big box, laying everything in there neatly. Our winter blankets were in the box, and I thought, *Well, that made sense. We wouldn't be needing them for awhile because it was springtime. Oh okay. She was putting away our winter stuff to make room for our spring stuff. That was all. Well, that made sense because she always seemed organized when it came to us.*

Ellie and I got bored and walked away to check out what might be going on at the other end of the pasture. We grazed for a little while. Then something else caught our attention. We looked up to see a truck pulling a large box on wheels down our gravel driveway. Ellie had no idea what it was because she had never seen one, but I had! I explained to Ellie that the large box on wheels carried horses and other animals around from one place to another. She looked puzzled, but eventually she started to understand its purpose.

Heather stopped what she was doing to greet the person who stepped out of the truck. It looked as if she knew him because

they gave each other a hug and she had a big smile on her face. I heard her tell the man, "Thank you," and he proceeded to walk into the house to greet Hugh.

Ellie and I looked at each other and then resumed our grazing. But we kept one eye on Heather as she returned to the room that contained all our things.

Why in the world would she need a big trailer like that if she were just doing some spring cleaning?

A few moments went by and we saw Heather emerge from the room with the big box she had been filling earlier. She opened the gate and walked over to the truck and trailer. She put the box on the backseat of the truck and shut the door. As the morning went on, she kept doing the same thing. She moved one box after another from our storage room to the truck. She started to look a bit weary, so she plopped down in the middle of the pasture to take a rest and have a sip of water.

Again—being the curious animals that we were—Ellie and I walked over to her and started sniffing around her as if to say, "What's going on here, Mommy?"

She just sat there for awhile as if to catch her breath. Once she did catch her breath, she blurted out to us that we were going on a trip. She looked really happy to tell us the news. And you can imagine how happy we were! Ellie and I stepped away from where Heather was sitting and started kicking, bucking,

and tossing our heads joyfully.

"We get to go! We get to go!" I exclaimed to Ellie.

Heather watched us celebrating and assumed that we could sense her happiness and, therefore, that we must have been happy too. I thought I heard her say, "Wow, they really understand!"

She wondered if it were the fact that a horse trailer had been hauled down the driveway or if it were that she had emptied all of our horsey stuff out of the storage room or if we really did understand what people were saying around us. At that moment, she didn't know which was the reason for our celebration. She was thrilled to be moving her entire family down south. We could see her excitement and could tell by her body language that she was over the moon with happiness. So were we!

Imagine all the new friends we were going to make in North Carolina. Imagine our big, green pasture there where we would be able to nibble on grass and gallop around together all we wanted. Think about all the new lessons we were going to learn as Mommy and Daddy learned more about us. We were staying together as a family, and I felt so lucky to be alive! We were very blessed indeed.

For the umpteenth time, I thought, *Thank you, Mommy and Daddy, for saving your little orphan many moons ago! I love you so much.*

"Get ready, Ellie, because we will be headed south, little girl!" I exclaimed to my little friend.

Sequoyah

Chapter 13

This is where I ended up after our move to the farm in North Carolina. Ellie and I had all our horsey things and a lot more space where we could run and explore.

There will be many more adventures and learning opportunities to come! And Ellie and I made some great new friends there too.

About the Author

Heather Rosselle Irwin has lived all over the country. She's resided in many settings, which include big cities, the country, and many places overseas. At the age of 12, she lived in Iran and was there during the Iranian revolution. As a result of the revolution, she and her family were evacuated out of the country in the middle of the night. They flew to Greece where they stayed for a few days. From there, she and her family traveled throughout Europe. That whole experience—while traumatic—allowed her to witness and live with adversity. When her dad asked the family where they wanted to live, they all voted to go back to the United States!

The events leading up to the evacuation from Iran were a torrential and potentially mind-blowing experience for her, but they're what gave her the strength and confidence to move forward and focus her life on what she loved.

※ ※ ※

Heather's heart belongs to the country life, to her husband, and to animals of all shapes and sizes. She's always worked with and around animals and has given them homes from the time she was able to walk and talk. At the age of 14, she started working for a veterinarian so she could work around animals and help them if she could. After that, she worked at a couple of pet shops and at a zoo for one summer. Her love for animals has led her to taking on her biggest challenge and responsibility, which was adopting and caring for her orphaned horse that she named Sequoyah.

※ ※ ※

In her 20s, she became a National Park Service Ranger after graduating from college with her BS degree in Parks and Recreation Management in

1988. She started her National Park Service job the following year. That was part of her dream.

Two things that have motivated Heather are the chances to step out of traditional roles for women and to pursue skills that women don't usually acquire. She was trained by the National Park Service and worked in cliff rescues, wildland fires, ocean rescues, and law enforcement as a National Park Service Ranger. She also conducted traffic and speed-enforcement duties during a lot of her assignments. She's ridden horses while patrolling Civil War battlefields.

Being a National Park Service Ranger afforded her the above opportunities as well as the opportunity to work outdoors, which she loves. Some of her responsibilities also included interpreting the history of the parks in which she was working and working in resource management as well. That included being aware of the park and its particular resources, protecting those resources through   educating the public and through law enforcement, and more. In some of the parks, these were natural resources. In other parks, they were cultural resources.

While she was growing up, Heather had dogs, cats, gerbils, hermit crabs, rabbits, a duck, a mouse, crayfish that she and her brother "fished" out of the creek, and other miscellaneous creatures that she loved. She never had a horse, but she always enjoyed horses through books and movies.

She got the opportunity to see what having a horse in her life would be like in the winter of 1999. The little horse—just two days old—became her responsibility in more ways than one. Not only would she become the keeper of this little baby, but also she would become its adoptive mother as well. The little horse that she named Sequoyah was orphaned from her real mother because her real mother didn't produce any milk for her. Sequoyah

was facing a battle for her life in her first two weeks, and Heather faced all kinds of changes and challenges in her life as a result of taking on the job of motherhood of this baby. Life changed dramatically for both of them forever!

Heather has always had a great love for and a deep connection with animals. She found yet another way she could help them, specifically horses and dogs. That was through Equine and Canine Sports Massage Therapy. She started doing massage therapy in 2003 when she completed her training and certification. Massage therapy helps the animals in a lot of different ways and pleases the animals and her greatly. That's another way she can continue to work around and spend meaningful time with these wonderful creatures!

www.ingramcontent.com/pod-product-compliance
Lightning Source LLC
LaVergne TN
LVHW010316070426
835513LV00021B/2408